Happiness is a Good Story: Finding Meaning in Life's Experiences

Nelle Moffett with Richard D. Bowers

Our personal stories shape our lives. Human beings were designed to create stories, make meaning, and interpret the world we perceive. This ability to make meaning defines our humanity as opposed to animals or plants. Our stories about ourselves and others are the meaning that we have made up to make sense of something that has happened. However, our suffering also lies primarily in the meaning that we have given to what has happened. If we assign the meaning to what happened, then we also are empowered to change the meaning that we create. To regain our empowerment, we have an opportunity to create stories that open up new possibilities, "re-frame" a situation, or re-tell our story to ourselves from a different framework. This book provides specific examples for how to transform your meaning-making process from one that is disempowering to one that empowers you as the hero of your own story.

Happiness is a Good Story

Finding Meaning in Life's Experiences

Other Books by Nelle Moffett and Richard D. Bowers

Taking Charge of Your Spiritual Path

Empathy in Conflict Intervention: The Key to Successful NVC Mediation

Happiness is a Good Story

Finding Meaning in Life's Experiences

Nelle Moffett
with Richard D. Bowers

Harmony World Publishing
Jerome, AZ

Copyright © 2013 by Nelle Moffett and Richard D. Bowers. All rights reserved. No part of this book may be reproduced or utilized in any form or by any means, electronic or mechanical, including photocopying, recording, or by any information storage and retrieval system, without permission in writing from the publisher.

Cover photograph by Richard D. Bowers.

Harmony World Publishing
PO Box 876
Jerome, AZ 86331-0876
Telephone: (805) 322-7476
www.harmonyworld.net

Printed in the United States of America

Trademarks: Nonviolent Communication, NVC, and The Center for Nonviolent Communication are trademarks of The Center for Nonviolent Communication located at 5600 San Francisco Rd. NE Suite A, Albuquerque, NM 87109.

ISBN 978-0-9911-1170-1

Acknowledgment

I acknowledge with much gratitude all of the people who have been my teachers, as well as the teachings and experiences that have contributed to the ideas I have expressed in this book including Marshall Rosenberg's Non-Violent Communication™, Ann Weiser Cornell's Inner Relationship Focusing, Landmark Education, Byron Katie's "The Work", *A Course in Miracles*, Cooperrider & Whitney's Appreciative Inquiry, Buddhism, Robert Kegan, Kennan Salinero, Sean Behr, and my experience teaching a college Psychology course on Sensation and Perception.

Table of Contents

	Preface	vii
Chapter 1	What Happened	1
Chapter 2	Starting at the Beginning	5
Chapter 3	Adding Meaning and Interpretation	13
Chapter 4	History and Memory	33
Chapter 5	Creating Enemies and Idols	39
Chapter 6	The Value of a Framework	47
Chapter 7	The Power of Stories	61
Chapter 8	Creating Empowering Stories	77
Chapter 9	Happiness is a Good Story	109
	About the Authors	121

Preface

This book is written by two authors, Nelle and Rick. We enjoy writing together and take on different roles in each book. We believe that using "I," rather than "we," is more personal and connecting with the reader. It is also much less awkward than shifting back and forth from "we" to "I" and creating ambiguity about which one of us is speaking. In this book, Nelle is the primary author using the word "I" to tell her stories from her perspective.

1

What Happened

Sara was very lonely as a child. Her two brothers and sister were older than she was by 10, 8, and 6 years. They were always off doing interesting things while Sara was still "too little" to participate. Sara's parents were also older than most, aged 45 when she was born. Consequently, she had the sense that her childhood energy was "too much" for them and had to be toned down. Sara was shy and spent a lot of time alone in her imaginary world. Her parents had high standards of perfection that Sara was expected to meet at an early age, and she didn't understand how her natural expressions were "not good enough" for them. Therefore

Sara grew up with a sense of being too little, too much to handle, and not good enough.

Heather was born into a privileged, white, middle class, educated, and spiritual family. She was the unexpected last child and therefore was made to feel that she was "special." Heather spent a lot of time around older children and adults and was included in their conversations.

She was encouraged to read, think, and express herself way beyond her years. Heather was "precocious and intelligent." As a child, Heather wanted to grow up to be the usual things for a girl: a ballerina, a teacher, a mother. However, Heather grew up without limitations about what a girl could do and the expectation that she could "be anything that she wanted to be." It was naturally expected that she would go to college, as both of her parents and all of her siblings had gone to college. Therefore Heather grew up with a sense of being special, intelligent, and able to be anything she wanted to be.

The interesting thing about these two very different upbringings is that they both occurred to the same person. These are stories about my childhood. Both stories are true in that they each contain verifiable facts, facts that others would agree about. They also both contain interpretations or perspectives that come from how I experienced the environment in which I grew up. This is what I will be talking about in this book, the difference between facts or observations on the one hand, and interpretations or perceptions on the other hand, and how understanding this difference can have a huge impact on one's life.

For many people, the difference between observation and interpretation is invisible in their daily living. Human beings tend to shift from one to the other so quickly that the two become blurred and blended together into one thing, which is perceived jointly as "what happened." In the case of my childhood experiences, I may have heard my mother say something like, "Keep your voice down." That is the observation. What I might have "heard" instead was, "You are annoying! Go away and stop being so annoying." This would have been my internal interpretation of what she said.

I will be making a case for separating these actions, making observations and making interpretations, into two discrete steps. By making this separation between observation and interpretation, I believe that we can regain our creative power as human beings.

2

Starting at the Beginning

In order to understand and distinguish observation from interpretation, it is helpful to know a little about how the brain works. This chapter is a short and hopefully painless course in Sensation and Perception that will provide a context for understanding what will follow. The main point I want to get across in this chapter is that human beings do not observe the world the way it is.

I will begin with a brief story about how human beings receive input about the world around us. In the beginning, as babies, we perceive the world around us as undifferentiated. Our senses of hearing, sight, taste, touch, and smell are still undeveloped and all jumbled together into a confusing soup of sensations. We have an innate ability to suckle and we put that to use immediately.

Gradually we begin to distinguish objects that are satisfying to suck on versus those that are not. We begin to distinguish the smell of familiar objects (people) and develop preferences and attachments to some over others. Our eyes begin to focus more on motion and our hands and legs interact with our environment in a way that allows us to distinguish and grab on to objects.

Fast forwarding, with the profound wisdom and guidance of nature we learn to sit, stand, walk, make sounds, recognize sounds, and eventually to form words and name objects.

Starting at the Beginning

We develop more and more refinement in being able to distinguish colors, categories, and varieties of ways to get our needs met. We begin to interact and communicate with the people in our world.

What is going on in our brains during this period is that we are learning what to do with the input received from the sensory organs: ears, eyes, tongue, nose, and skin. The brain is developing neuronal networks that translate the sensory input into meaningful data. The upside-down undifferentiated blur that the eyes receive is translated into right-side-up images with edges, shapes, names, uses, and values. The same is occurring with all of the other sensory input.

Our brains learn how to interpret the sensory input both from our direct interactions with our environment and from indirect interactions through the people who are transmitting their interpretations. For example, we experience a dog through touching the fur, feeling the wet tongue lick our cheek, and seeing the dog moving in the space around us. We also hear our mother call the dog "daw-gy," or "bow-wow," or in Spanish, "perrito." Sometimes when we say "daw-gy" our mother says, "No, caaat, caaat" and we may be confused about what just happened. Gradually we build an understanding of our world and the language to describe what we are sensing.

We learn which sensory input is important and which to ignore or filter out. After all, there is a huge amount of sensory input to attend to and much of it is simply not needed. For instance, we learn the sounds that are used in our native language and we lose the ability to hear or distinguish sounds that are not used in our language. We learn what objects are used for, what categories go together, what is acceptable, what to avoid, what we like and don't like.

Our sensory experience of the world is not a direct replica of the world "out there." For example, we do not see with our eyes like a video camera. We "see" with the brain, which goes through a process of filtering, flipping, organizing, recognizing, and categorizing the input from the eyes. That which is not important is not seen. The input is rearranged to match a learned schema of how things should be. The brain has learned how to organize the input into meaningful objects that are recognized and to group this input with similar input learned from the past. From the beginning, sensory input is already "contaminated" by the meaning that our brains give to it in order to select, perceive, store, name, and apply what we are sensing.

Developments in quantum physics add even more uncertainty to the world that we experience by proposing that there is no way to identify the true state of the world, but I will not be going to that level in this discussion. My focus here is on the world as we generally experience it. On one level, the distinction between observation and interpretation is meaningless because our observations are already full of meaning that has been added.

However, there is still value in getting as close to "pure" observation on one hand and interpretation on the other hand to be able to unravel the rampant confusion that I see in the way people speak about their experiences. Examples of this confusion can be seen in relationships, conflicts, historical accounts, religions, politics, law, newspapers, textbooks, movies, etc.. The confusion I am referring to is confusion between what happened and the meaning and interpretation that is added to what happened. I will be providing several examples of observations and interpretations throughout this book to clarify this distinction.

3

Adding Meaning and Interpretation

Let's start by distinguishing between observations and interpretations. Observations describe what happened in a way that a video camera or a "fly on the wall" would register: what can be seen, heard, smelled, tasted, or felt on the skin. Observations could be direct quotes of what someone said, behavior that is observed like a smile, rolling the eyes, pacing back and forth, or something that can be measured like the temperature of the room shown on the thermometer, etc.

Interpretations, by contrast, are judgments or meaning added about the observations. For example look at the difference between these statements:

- you are angry,

- your face is red and you are frowning, so I am guessing that you are angry.

The first statement is an example of interpretation and it does not contain any observation to show what led to the interpretation. This statement is said in a way that assumes that the observer's interpretation is the truth about another person.

The second statement has two observations followed by the interpretation that was made. This statement provides feedback about what was observed and then acknowledges the interpretation as a guess about the other

Adding Meaning and Interpretation 15

person rather than the truth. The second statement allows for correction: "No, I am not angry. I feel embarrassed."

What follows is a discussion of three common examples of how we add meaning and interpretation in our communications, often without being aware of doing so: mind reading, speculation, and judgment.

Mind Reading

In mind reading, the person speaking or narrating assigns intentions or thoughts to another person as if it is the truth about that person. This might occur in a newspaper article in which the author says, "Politician X voted against bill xyz because she is against the environment." How politician X voted is a matter of public record and verifiable as either correctly or incorrectly reporting the fact. Why politician X voted the way she did is not known unless there is a direct quote from politician X indicating the reason for her vote. In that case, using the quote and citing its source would be staying in observation and out of interpretation. Asserting that one knows the reason why politician X voted the way she did overlooks the possibility that politicians sometimes vote down a bill they would normally be in favor of because it is not well specified, has riders that are contrary to their values, there is no funding to support the bill, or any number of other reasons that may or may not be public.

Here is another example of mind reading that may be closer to home. I have a friend whose teenage son got an opportunity to volunteer to accompany police officers in their squad cars on the job. He got to wear a uniform and a badge. When the son started talking about wanting to be a policeman, my friend was concerned that his son enjoyed the adrenaline

Adding Meaning and Interpretation   17

and macho energy, and that is why he wanted to join the police force. My friend was assuming that he knew his son's motivation. However, when he expressed his concern to his son, the son replied that he wanted to be a policeman because he wanted to be around people who help others, and he wanted to be a part of that. This was not at all what the father expected!

Another example is a father who came home tired from work, and his son charged into the house full of energy. The father told his son, "Hold on, slow down, and sit quietly until I get my boots off." The son obeyed his father and waited as patiently as he could. When his father said he could speak now, the son blurted out, "Mrs. Smith told me to run over and tell you that her kitchen is on fire!" What assumptions had the father been making about his son in this instance?

What about the wife who thinks her husband doesn't trust her with money and is stingy because he won't let her get her own checking account? They argue about this for years before they have a conversation in which he is able to express his concern about their financial well-being, and explains that he is trying to manage their limited resources the best he can to save up to buy a house for her. This is very different from the intention that the wife made up about her husband!

A person I knew bought a used RV and afterwards discovered that the water pump didn't work. He immediately assumed that the seller had lied to him and he had been taken advantage of. He was intensely angry and wanted revenge. It didn't occur to him that there might be another perspective. The RV had been in storage for a long period of time, and the seller may not have known the status of every system in the RV. The price might have been a fair price even if there were some things that needed repair. He might have remembered that he had tested many of the systems in the RV but had failed to test the water system, and therefore he could have taken responsibility for his own oversight.

What about news about current events? Do we really know what terrorists were thinking and intending? Do we know what bankers, loan officers, or financial investors intended before the financial collapse? Do we know what soldiers in the military, chemists in pharmaceutical companies, or executives in industrial companies are thinking when they go to work? Do we even know for sure what we would be thinking or intending if we were in their shoes?

A more dangerous example of mind reading occurred in the Cuban missile crisis. The way I understand what happened is that the Americans were interpreting the moves of the Russians as meaning they intended to attack. The Russians were interpreting the actions of the Americans as meaning that we were going to attack. The actions of each side led to an escalation of action by the other side.

The crisis was avoided when President Kennedy took a gamble and changed his interpretation of the Russian's actions, guessing that they didn't want to engage in a battle any more than he did. Kennedy ordered an action that would clearly signal that we were backing off. The Russians correctly interpreted the move and also backed off, and the crisis was averted. How easily it could have gone the other way!

Whether or not this is an accurate portrayal of what happened in this historic event, we likely don't know. I certainly wasn't in the room

Adding Meaning and Interpretation 21

when these decisions were being made. However, I offer this story as an example of what could happen when assumptions are made by opposing sides about what the other side is thinking. Human beings can create an interpretation about what is going on, get all heated up about what they have made up about the other person's intentions without checking it out, and then act as if their interpretation is the truth. In the Cuban missile crisis event, Kennedy may have had the wisdom to realize that assumptions were being made about the intentions of the Russians, and had the courage to test out these assumptions before acting on them.

The point of these examples is to show how common it is that we think we know what others are thinking. But we really don't know what they are thinking unless we ask. Most of us cannot read minds. With people that we know and live with, we are more likely to discover their intentions sooner or later. However, with strangers, public officials, bosses, or others where communication is constrained or nonexistent, we can continue to believe we know what they are thinking without ever checking it out to discover what is true.

In the absence of real information from the source, we tend to *believe* our assumptions about what other people are thinking. **Our assumptions are nothing more than stories that we have made up in a vacuum of current information.**

When I say that we tend to make up something, I do not mean that we intentionally fabricate something that is not true or that we are telling a lie. This would imply that we know what is true but choose instead to say something that we know is not true. What I am

Adding Meaning and Interpretation 23

describing is the inherently human trait of making meaning where none exists or filling in gaps where information is missing. In the case of mind reading, we make up what we believe the other person is thinking or intending and then act as if that is the truth.

Philosophers and psychologists have claimed that meaning-making is what human beings do automatically. Just as we do not simply receive sensory input intact but instead interpret and make meaning out of the sensory input, human beings live within a narrative life story and will fill in the gaps when the details are missing. This is so common that we don't notice when we do it and usually don't notice when someone else does it unless we are aware of the facts ourselves.

Have you ever had a newspaper article written about you or about something that you know well? It has been surprising to me to see the number of errors that show up in these articles! Articles about events we are familiar with are probably not the only articles with errors, but we tend to accept other articles at face value when we don't know the facts and can't spot the errors. Human beings love a good story!

Speculation

The second common example of adding meaning and interpretation is speculation. One form of speculation is inventing a story about what will happen in the future based on incomplete facts or information. It is my experience in relationships and work environments that making up something to fill a vacuum of information is a common occurrence. For example, when management does not communicate to the workers, rumors spread like wildfire.

Adding Meaning and Interpretation

The problem about speculation, in the context of this discussion, is when it is used to make meaning and is then believed to be true rather than being someone's opinion. Next time there are national elections, listen to the newscasters and make a tally of how often they report a verifiable fact (i.e., a quote, an event that has occurred in time and place, an event that is scheduled to occur, or actual counts from polls), and how many times they are speculating about who is likely to win the primary, expressing opinions without labeling them as opinions, or weaving a story about what will happen if this person drops out of the race, etc.. I think you will find that most of the air waves are taken up with speculation. But don't just accept my speculative guess as the truth; do a count and find out for yourself if this is true or not!

Another form of speculation is declaring a certain outcome before it has occurred. This is a case where a person is convinced beyond a doubt that if event "A" happens, event "B" will certainly be the result. A harmless example is a woman who sees her son going out without a jacket and says, "You are going to catch your death of cold!"

Other examples are not so harmless. Human beings can hold these absolute predictions so tightly and be so convinced of the truth and inevitability of them that there is no way to convince them of other possible outcomes. These intractable predictions are so firmly believed that people will fight to defend them, even if it is not in their own best interest to believe them, and even if there is plenty of evidence to show that the feared outcome is not certain to occur. Maybe you know someone who has an irrational prediction like this. It is much easier to see the irrational nature of these predictions in someone else than in our own treasured predictions.

Let me tentatively propose a few of these intractable predictions, hoping that I don't tread on one of yours.

- A student might believe that if he gets a "C" in this college course that his life is ruined.

- A teenage girl might believe that if her boyfriend leaves her, she will never find anyone as good as he is again.

- An elderly woman believes that if she moves into a senior home, her children will never come to visit her.

- A man believes that if his son joins the military, he will certainly be killed.

- I was told by a statistics professor that if I dropped out of college before getting my degree, that I would never finish my degree. (I didn't believe him, dropped out, and later finished two more degrees.)

As with mind reading, the problem with speculation is that we create a story and then we forget that we made it up. We act as if the story is true. We share the story with our friends and co-workers, we get elated or depressed based on the story, and we make decisions based on the story, all without being aware that it is just a story and not the truth.

Judgment

A third kind of meaning and interpretation we add is judgment. When we observe something happening, human beings tend to add meaning to the event that is not contained in the event

Adding Meaning and Interpretation

itself. Events are, in themselves, neutral. But human beings tend to add in a judgment about the positive or negative nature of the event or what the event means about us or another person. Let's look at some examples.

- Linda's daughter is reprimanded at school for talking in class. Linda feels embarrassed because she adds that this means she is not a good mother.

- John gets a letter of admission to college before any of his friends. He feels proud because he adds that this means he is smarter than his friends.

- Barbara is promoted at work to an executive position. Her friend Joan feels jealous because she adds that this means that Barbara is more successful than Joan.

- Bobby's mother does not attend the annual parent/teacher conference at his school. Bobby feels sad and angry because he adds that this means his mother doesn't care about him as much as the other kids' mothers care about their kids.

- Dan's landlord has not fixed the heater in his apartment despite repeated requests. Dan feels angry because he has added the meaning that his landlord is lazy, greedy, and doesn't care about the well-being of his tenants.

Each of these examples shows that a person has added a judgment to the event that happened. The judgment is not inherent in the event, but is created from the person's interpretation of the event. The same event can be interpreted in many different ways by different people. This is what is meant by an event being

Adding Meaning and Interpretation 31

neutral, in itself. In fact, the same event can be interpreted differently by the same person given a change in perspective.

There is a well-known story about a man who has a son. The son buys a wonderful horse. The neighbors praise the good fortune of the son, but the man simply says, "We'll see." The son is out riding the horse and gets thrown off and breaks his leg. The neighbors tell the father how unfortunate his son is to have broken his leg, but the father replies, "We'll see." Shortly afterward, the army comes through town and enlists all able-bodied young men. They do not take the son because he has a broken leg. The neighbors tell the man how fortunate he is that the army did not take his son, but the father replies, "We'll see."

In this story, the neighbors are constantly adding meaning to the events that occur, saying how fortunate or unfortunate they are. The father stays with the events themselves, neither judging them nor predicting where they will lead. The father wisely waits for events to unfold without adding any meaning to them.

This is a story used to teach students about the human tendency to judge our circumstances. It is useful as a teaching story to build awareness, but not necessarily as a model to emulate for most of us. Instead, it is useful to help us begin to notice how much we judge our circumstances as either positive or negative.

4

History and Memory

Human beings do not only add interpretation and meaning in present events. If we look closely, we can see that historical descriptions and memory have more to do with the stories that we create than with the events that happened.

In our personal pasts, what we remember most is our judgments about what happened rather than the details about what occurred. What we remember about the distant past has usually been so processed and changed that we no longer know what really happened. We remember the stories that we have told repeatedly about how the past was for us. We then react to the meaning that we gave to the past events rather than to the events themselves.

When I work with individuals in conflict resolution, I will ask them to describe what happened that stimulated the conflict. In one example, the person replied, "He lied!" When I asked again, what happened, he said, "He sold me this used motorcycle and he knew it didn't work!" This person was not able to recount the events that happened between the parties. All he was able to do was to pronounce his judgments and interpretations of what happened.

Going to the seller, I got the details of the events. The seller had dated receipts showing that the particular part in question had been replaced including the ID number of the motorcycle. He said that the buyer had test driven the motorcycle before buying it. He had shown the buyer all of the repair and maintenance receipts he had on the motorcycle and given the buyer copies when he purchased the motorcycle. The motorcycle was sold "As is" on the sales receipt. When I shared this description of what had happened with the buyer, he agreed that these were the facts of what happened. He then replied, "This guy is a liar!"

The human brain stores the events of our past in episodic memory. In other words, we record the story we told ourselves about what happened. We do not store an exact transcript or video of the actual events. We experienced the events from our own perspective and level of understanding at the time and our memory reflects this point of view.

Over time, we also recreate our past with re-interpretations from more current perspectives, adding meaning that we weren't even capable of making at the time the events occurred. We most likely didn't know, at the time we stored these events, what were the perspectives and motivations of the other people involved, but our memory will contain our added interpretations and judgments about their motivations. We will remember how we felt and most likely our brain will fill in the gap of missing information to create a story that makes sense from our perspective.

We don't know that we are doing this, and when we recall something from the past, we often cannot distinguish what occurred and what we have added. Very often the details will be vague, but the feelings and meaning we made will be remembered as "what happened." This recreation of our own history is a common human experience even though we are mostly unaware that we do this.

History and Memory

Even written history of world events is not simply recounting what happened. Historical accounts are narratives from the particular perspective of the person telling the story. For instance, Native Americans have challenged the story of Columbus "discovering" America as representing the event from a Eurocentric perspective that is certainly different from the Native American perspective. The "winners" usually get to write the history books from their own perspective, while purporting to be telling the facts of "what happened!"

Events are often recorded around the time they occur, but from a particular person's point of view. Sometimes though, the history is written many years, decades, or centuries after the actual events took place. Not all events and perspectives are recorded, just some of them. Some records may even have been lost prior to a historical account being written.

In addition to these various sources of inaccuracy or one-sided perspective, the historical events are not even interesting in themselves. What makes them interesting is that someone interprets why these events are important. Historians select from the existing records of what happened only those details that they decide are the most important for the story that they are telling. They will then thread the events together, filling in the gaps with guesses, opinions, and interpretations to make a particular point. In other words, historians write a feasible story, from a particular perspective, based on selected records among those that exist, to relate the events in a meaningful and interesting way. Human beings do love a good story!

5

Creating Enemies and Idols

In the previous chapter, I described various ways that human beings add interpretation and meaning to events that happen. Another important example of interpretation and meaning-making occurs in the way that human beings create enemy and idol images of people and then believe that this is the truth about them. The process of creating enemy images of people is especially damaging when it is used to make wars acceptable.

Let's look at how human beings create these false images of people. I believe that we can observe and agree that human beings are a combination of positive and negative traits. We share more in common with each other than differences. Underneath all appearances, we all want to be loved. However, when we do not receive the love that we want, we will usually attack either ourselves or others. On a personal level, enemies and idols are images that we create about people, based in part on whether we receive the love we want, and then we believe that this is who they are.

An inward attack will take the form of noticing and expanding all of the negative qualities about our self that explain why we did not receive the love we wanted. We will create a story about our self that says, "if only I were not so unworthy, I would have received the love I wanted."

An outward attack will take the form of noticing and expanding all of the negative qualities about the other person who did not give us the love that we expected. We will create a story about this person that will justify our anger. We will create this person in the image of a villain and create our self as an undeserving victim. We will tell our self that, "if only the other person were not such a bad person, they would see how badly they behaved and how much I deserve better treatment."

Creating Personal Enemies and Idols

There is a mental process we go through to create an enemy image of a person. In both inward and outward attack, our memory becomes very focused and selective. We will see only those examples that support the enemy image and ignore any evidence to the contrary. In other words, our attention becomes constricted in order to justify our attack. We therefore believe that we are seeing our enemies accurately for who they are, rather than as a fabrication in our own mind. After all, we have "proof" of how stupid, inconsiderate, selfish, immoral, or evil they are.

The process of creating idol images occurs in the same way. We can either create an idol of our self or of others. In either case, our memory becomes very focused and selective of the good qualities of our self or the other person. We will see only those examples of saintly behavior, selflessness, generosity, long enduring patience, self-discipline, wisdom, unconditional love, and higher consciousness. We create a story based on all of the evidence we have accumulated to support the pedestal upon which we have placed our idols. We believe that we are seeing our idols accurately for who they are, rather than as a fabrication in our own mind. We have "proof" of their superiority and worthiness of our esteem.

In both stories, enemy image and idol image, the evidence we find is real. We have most likely truly observed the behaviors that demonstrate these qualities in all the detail that we remember. Even if we ignore all of the meaning and interpretation that we have likely added to our observations, the problem is that our mind is supplying us with only partial evidence. In the process of creating an enemy or an idol, there is another side of the evidence that is ignored or suppressed. In other words, in the case of our idols, we ignore their foibles and, in the case of our enemies, we ignore their contributions. If we are playing the role of proving guilt, the mind will comply and provide that evidence. If we are trying to proclaim innocence and exaltation, the mind will likewise comply with the appropriate evidence.

Creating Collective Enemies and Idols

Creating enemy or idol images on a larger scale occurs in much the same way as our personal process. As social groups of human beings, we also collectively create enemy or idol images of other sexes, cultures, races, religions, and countries. In fact, human beings seem to be prone to identifying in-groups and out-groups and creating an "other" out there to worship or hate.

I once worked with a client who was a staunch environmentalist. She was an active leader on local, state, and national levels. Because of her strong beliefs, she had created enemy images of people who seemingly caused environmental problems, or people who failed to support

Creating Enemies and Idols

environmental protections in the way that she wanted them to. She recognized that, to be effective, she needed to be able to communicate with people in positions of power. However, as much as she wanted to, she had a hard time letting go of the enemy image she had of these people enough to be able to communicate with them in respectful ways.

Some of the news media are particularly prone to creating enemy images of groups of people that breed fear and justify incarcerating or killing people who fit into this feared group. Prior to waging war, it is common to observe the political leadership creating an enemy image of the other as "inhuman" in order to justify killing them.

And yet if we sat down with these people who have been characterized as "inhuman", we would likely find that they are human beings just like us, with hopes and dreams, positive and negative qualities, and a desire to live in safety with their families. We would discover that they also have an enemy image of us that is not the truth about us. Both sides are operating out of stories of each other that were made up but are assumed to be the truth about the other.

6

The Value of a Framework

There is nothing wrong with creating a story, with making meaning, or with interpreting the world we perceive. This is what human beings, as opposed to animals or plants, were designed to do. This ability to make meaning defines our humanity. We cannot stop creating meaning and still retain what we recognize as being human. We will continue to make meaning, interpret our sensory input, and create stories. Humans not only love a good story, they cannot thrive without one.

Human beings are constantly trying to understand, categorize, and name the world we live in. Have you ever heard of someone who had an illness that could not be diagnosed? They sometimes report feeling such anguish about not knowing what illness they have. They search and search and go from doctor to doctor trying to discover what they have. Finally they may have found a doctor that says, "You have an extremely rare disease called 'hrqlkhrwer.' We don't know much about it, but I will work with you to try different things and see what helps you." The person then reports feeling relief that now they finally have a name for the disease they have, even though they haven't received any remedy for the disease!

There is something powerfully satisfying about having a name or category into which we can put our human experience. These categorizations and names are not inherent in the things themselves. Some quantum physicists and spiritual teachers might even object to using the word "things" to describe our encounters in the world since even the boundaries around which we define something is a human construction.

Human Beings Need Frameworks

There is a story about two spiritual masters who met for tea one day. The masters sipped their tea together in silence, while their disciples stood at a respectful distance. At one point, one of the masters spoke up and said, "They call that a 'tree!'" whereupon both masters laughed uproariously.

Again, this is a teaching story used to illustrate the human process of naming and categorizing our sensory input. We don't need to get that abstract to recognize that we have many languages in the world that apply different labels to things. We also have different branches of scientific, theological, medical, social, and political systems that categorize and label things differently and create different stories, theories, orientations, or frameworks for understanding the phenomena that they observe.

This is not a trivial process. Human beings need an orientation or framework in order to perceive the world and interact with it. Without a framework that provides meaning, we will not even perceive the world. Said in a different way, we will only perceive that which we can connect to an existing framework; everything else will be invisible.

An example from my own life, from my college years, occurred when my mechanically oriented brother came to visit me. My vacuum cleaner wasn't working and I asked if he could fix it. He got out his tools and, while I watched, he magically opened it up. I say "magically" because up until that point, I had somehow missed noticing that things can be taken apart. He showed me the screws that held the case together. I had never perceived screws before! They had been completely invisible to me. All of a sudden, I began to notice screws everywhere! Light switch plates have screws in them! Toasters have screws in them! Book shelves have screws in them! I was now empowered in the world in a way I had never been, when screws were invisible.

Another example of an empowering framework for me was when I learned about the Enneagram method of categorizing various personality patterns (like the Myers-Briggs, True Colors, and other personality typing schemas). Before I learned this method of noticing patterns among people, I was mystified by people. All people were an undistinguished blur in my mind. I couldn't see any patterns that made sense and therefore, I couldn't understand why someone might do what they did and was caught off guard without any way of understanding the world of people around me.

When I learned about the Enneagram, suddenly I could see patterns, similar to the appearance of screws in my life. People began to make sense to me. I could understand why certain people might clash, what common core issues people might have, and how people can develop along a visible path. I began to recognize my own pattern in myself. I also began to recognize other people with the same pattern as mine, and I didn't feel so alone and odd. I had a basis for connection and compassion with others that didn't exist before.

The Enneagram framework gave me a way to understand and make sense of my experiences with people that had previously been so confusing. Having a framework is not only satisfying and empowering; it is also essential for our ability to perceive and make sense of the world.

So a framework is an essential way that we see the world. Now here is a challenging question: Is a framework the Truth? Is the Enneagram the Truth? My answer is, no the Enneagram is no more the Truth than "tree" is the Truth. Both the Enneagram and "tree" are incomplete attempts to describe something; they are both stories that we human beings have made up to make sense of our world. They could have been made up differently and actually have been formulated into different frameworks.

The Enneagram is one among many different personality typing systems, each creating different category groupings and naming different aspects of human patterns, and each one making visible a different view of a person. "Tree" is used to describe things as varied as a palm tree, a maple tree, and a giant Sequoia. It would be interesting to speculate about how the object that western culture perceives as a "tree" might be perceived differently by a New Zealand Maori or an Alaskan Eskimo. My guess is that their perceptions may be as different from each other and our own view of a tree as that of the spiritual masters or even the view of "tree" fantasized in the movie Avatar!

Let's look at an even more challenging area where frameworks or stories play an important part in human understanding, and that is religion. Each religion around the world has its own version of the story of creation. Since human beings were not around to have actually observed creation at the start, it is not too difficult to rationalize that these creation stories were made up in an attempt to make sense of our world and to define the place of human beings in that world.

Just like children asking, "Where do I come from," we seem to need a framework for understanding our origin. Religious teachers, just like historians, create a narrative full of meaning out of limited historical "evidence" and oral traditions to provide followers with an orientation for understanding their place in the world and their relationship to a creator, the creation, and to other human beings. A religious framework or orientation provides a sense of safety in the world as well as a way of understanding our purpose and role.

Science provides a secular version of the creation story. Like religious leaders and historians, scientists create a narrative full of meaning out of limited "evidence" and often conflicting theories to provide followers with an orientation for understanding how the world works. Science defines the purpose and role of each aspect of the material world and the interrelationships among them. A scientific framework or orientation provides a sense of safety in the world, a way to predict how the material world will respond in different circumstances, and therefore provides human beings with a sense of control over their environment.

Without an orientation of some kind, whether religious or secular, human beings feel disoriented, lost, rudderless, adrift, despairing, and may even lose touch with any sense of grounding or connection with themselves or the world. Human beings consider this sense of orientation and grounding to be of such importance and essential to being a fully functioning human being that some would label the absence of this state as "insane." Human beings need a good story in order to feel grounded and secure in their humanity!

Limitations of Frameworks

While frameworks are necessary for human development, they also can become a limitation. As with interpretation and meaning-making, frameworks are stories that we create, and then we often forget that we created them. When a framework becomes seen as the Truth, rather than a man-made theory, we lose empowerment and perspective. We draw lines in the sand and create enemies out of people who are using a framework that is different from our own. We fight wars and kill people in defense of our made-up frameworks.

When we have connected to relationships or communities who share our particular framework, it becomes doubly hard to see the man-made origin of the framework. Community members mutually reinforce their framework. Communities create a sense of belonging by having a shared framework. A member of the community receives reinforcement for believing in the framework of the community.

Furthermore, the community enforces loyalty to the framework through either an implied or overtly stated threat of expulsion from the community if a member questions or deviates from the common framework. For instance, scientists or professors who want to conduct research in areas that are not part of the

The Value of a Framework   59

framework of their intellectual community put their reputation and careers in jeopardy. Husbands or wives who want to explore a different way of framing their world from their partner put their marriages and mutual friendships at risk. Adult children who want to adopt a different framework from their parents may be estranged from their families.

While frameworks offer a way for making sense of our world and providing security and belonging, they also can become too small.

A friend of mine commented, "Exactly! I attended a friendly and cozy church for some years that was home to many good and sincere people. Its strong sense of community and small-town values were nostalgically comforting to me. I finally had to decide to leave, a sad day for me, but philosophically necessary. It became apparent to me that the framework of belief, or world view, of the minister, was entirely appropriate to a small homogeneous suburban town which loved its own illustrious past, but too narrow in its charming, simple small-town values, to offer me solutions to the big-city issues that confronted me in my daily life at my college classes at a large urban university." C.F., 2013, Personal communication.

We may limit our personal and community potential for development by remaining "loyal" to a framework. When we make frameworks rigid and fixed rather than fluid and evolving, we begin to serve frameworks instead of using frameworks to serve our humanity. Einstein's definition of insanity is to continue doing the same thing while expecting a different result. Rather than grounding us in our sanity, frameworks can sometimes lock us into our insanity.

7

The Power of Stories

It is inevitable and needed for human beings to operate within frameworks which are created to make sense of our world. We start out when we are children with a Santa Claus or Cinderella story which gets updated, refined, and developed into more adult models that apply to the worlds of family, career, religion, politics, health, and more. These frameworks are useful. We couldn't operate without them. They are modified often through our life span to fit new information from our life experience, education, or developmental level. The important point here is that, while stories are essential, they are also changeable.

In the first chapter, I stated that human beings tend to shift from observation to interpretation so quickly that the two become blurred and blended together into one thing, which is perceived jointly as "what happened." I have provided the groundwork to distinguish the difference between observation and interpretation, and to justify the importance and inevitability of both processes as part of the human experience. I now want to present a case for separating these actions into two distinct steps.

I believe that we regain our creative power as human beings when we learn to make this separation between observation and interpretation because we open up many more choices for our actions. For example, the ways that we describe and interpret what has happened in our world can create either an empowering or a disempowering story. Our stories are not just passive descriptions of how we experience the world; our stories and the language we use to describe our experiences can actually determine the world we experience.

Language is Generative

First, let's look at how our language and the stories or frameworks we use can be generative. The term generative means that the words and frameworks we use produce a certain kind of outcome based on the nature of the words and frameworks. Words generate an outcome of the same kind as the quality and nature of the words themselves. Let's look at the process that creates this generative relationship between words/frameworks and outcomes.

We have already looked at several examples that show how human beings develop through a process of selecting, naming, categorizing, and interpreting the meaning of our world. Through a process of acculturation from the environment in which we grow up, meaning has been crucial in each step of perception, not just added on at the end. Selection of which sensory input to attend to and which to ignore is based on a learned meaning of the importance of various input. Things that are not important are not perceived and do not get a name or category. They simply do not exist in our framework at all. Once perceived, the name becomes understood as the thing itself. When we equate the object with its name, the name becomes the meaning assigned to the object. Once named, it is placed into categories with similar meanings.

Therefore, what we call something determines how it is judged, categorized, and used. It also will generate where we look for other similar things; we will look under the same category as

The Power of Stories

the thing itself. For example, the way we name a problem will generate only certain types of solutions that "fit" the problem. For example, in an organization, like Enron or Countrywide, if we say that the problem is incompetent employees, solutions will focus on counseling and maybe firing those employees. However, the same problem could be identified as a lack of communication or cooperation between units and solutions will be sought in that arena. The problem could also be seen as a failure of leadership and those responsible would likely be replaced. Or further, the problem could be seen as a result of problems in how the system is designed and systemic solutions would be pursued. The point is, how the problem is named will generate what comes next.

To see this more clearly, perhaps a counter example would be useful. In some circles, there is a phrase "out-of-the-box-thinking."

This phrase points to a practice of looking at things outside of the usual categorization, outside of their normal function, purpose, and assigned meaning. To do this requires a suspension of the already-made meaning which allows for the creation of a new meaning, purpose, and function.

I remember hearing about an exercise in a design school that required students to use an assortment of given objects, (i.e., matches, rubber band, pencil, etc.) to create a specified outcome. The solution to this exercise required that some of the objects be used in ways that are different from their normal function. This exercise was designed to teach students how to find creative solutions to problems by seeing things from a different perspective.

The language we use and the meaning, framework, or story we tell, place things and experiences in our world into categories that define their meaning, purpose, and function. To change the meaning, purpose, and function of something, we often must change the language and framework we use to allow for out-of-the-box creativity to be more accessible. In this way, the stories we tell are generative of what we will see and the possibilities that will be accessible to us.

Here is a story to illustrate how this works. I have a friend, I'll call her Carol, who was divorced and, after a period of time, was beginning to date again. Carol was clear about wanting to find a man who had a spiritual practice, was a mature adult who had worked out most of his "issues," and who was ready for a relationship that was a mutual partnership.

When a man, let's call him Martin, from within her own spiritual tradition asked her on a date, she was at first amazed and excited. Then Carol's critical mind set in and her mind began to point out all of his flaws. She created a story that "he is wrong for me." Given her experience in her previous marriage, it is not at all surprising that a voice of caution would show up. However, she realized that if she continued to see Martin as "wrong for her" that her mind would prove that she was right in this judgment.

Instead Carol created a story for herself that it was "possible" that Martin was exactly what she was looking for. Notice that she did not create a story that he was in fact right for her; she just opened herself to a possibility that he <u>might</u> be right for her. This allowed her mind to receive a broader range of evidence so that she could get a more complete picture of who Martin was.

Carol did actually discover that she and Martin were very compatible and that he had the qualities that she was looking for. After a slow and careful development of their relationship, they were married. Carol is convinced that if she had not changed her story, she would have rejected Martin without discovering the kind of person he really was.

Disempowering and Empowering Stories

Notice that in the example above, Carol started with the story, "he is wrong for me." This story was not based on real observations but on her inner fears of making a mistake again. If Carol had lived within this story, she would likely not have allowed a chance to get real experience and make real observations of Martin. She would have allowed her fears, assumptions, and pre-judgments to determine the outcome. Carol would not have stayed connected with Martin long enough to collect a balanced set of observations in a variety of circumstances so that she could make an informed choice. This is an example of what I would call creating a disempowering story. It is disempowering because, by living in this story, Carol would have remained a victim of her past experience and fears.

When Carol created the story of "he is possibly right for me," she created an inquiry, an opening to gather an array of evidence, to discover Martin's qualities from her direct experience of him. In this way she created an "empowering" story which gave her openness to possibility and choice. She was no longer a victim, but rather an explorer and an autonomous agent acting on her own behalf.

The Power of Stories

Disempowering stories are rampant in the world. Disempowering stories include stories of oneself as a victim, stories that depict others or oneself as weak, small, or incapable, stories that perceive the world as fixed or against me, and stories that identify all the reasons something won't work.

These stories are disempowering because they deny or ignore the source of the stories. When we create meaning and then forget that we made it up and feel trapped in it, we have disowned our source of power. However, when we begin to take responsibility for our story-making, we can turn our world around.

One kind of disempowering story is one in which we characterize ourselves through self-limiting stories. For example, how frequently do you hear yourself or others saying things like, I can't sing, I am not a social person, I am no good at math, I am all thumbs when it comes to mechanical things. These kinds of statements are really just stories that we have made up about ourselves and are not necessarily the truth about us.

I have a friend who frequently said, "I can never remember people's names." Someone pointed out to him that this was just a story he had made up about himself and that he could change his story if he wanted to. By living into this self-limiting story, at least two things happened. One, he didn't bother to try to remember names, since he wasn't any good at it; he didn't pay attention when people said their name. Second, he only noticed the times when he didn't remember someone's name and then repeated his mantra, "I am no good at remembering people's names."

When he was told that this is just a story he made up about himself, he decided to change his story to, "I am great at remembering names." Again, at least two things happened. He began to pay more attention when people said their names and he noticed when he did remember people's names, repeating his new mantra about himself, "I am great at remembering people's names." Through changing his self-limiting story to one that was more empowering, he found that he was able to remember people's names more often.

Another friend considered herself to be really awkward in social situations. Someone pointed out to her that she was probably just as capable in social situations as she was in anything else that she put her attention to doing. Perhaps it wasn't that she was inadequate in some way, but rather that she wasn't interested in what was going on in these situations. In other words, this person offered my friend a new story about her experience in social settings.

My friend realized that this new story was actually as true, or perhaps even more true, than the story she had been telling herself. She changed her story to one that was more empowering: "When I am not interested in what is happening in a social setting, I generally choose not to participate." This new story empowered her to either change her choice, change her circumstance, or just accept that she is currently not interested in what is going on without making it mean that there was something deficient about herself. She also found that when she was interested in what was going on in a social gathering, she was very much able to participate and engage with the interactions.

Understanding the Source of Suffering

Our stories about ourselves and others are the meaning that we have made up to make sense of something we have observed. Our suffering lies primarily in the meaning that we give to what has happened. Many wise teachers have said that it is not the specific problem that causes our suffering but rather it is our thoughts or meaning-making about the problem that causes our suffering.

It is so easy to feel at the mercy of the world when we are not aware of the difference between our observations and interpretations. When these two actions become merged together, we believe that we are perceiving the world as it is rather than as we have interpreted it. We confuse what happened with the meaning that we gave to what happened.

Realizing this confusion of processes can become the source of empowerment over our suffering. If we didn't believe the self-limiting stories we tell, what would be possible for us in our lives? If we didn't believe the limiting stories we tell about others, what would be possible in our relationships?

It is not simply a matter of getting rid of stories. Remember that human beings make meaning automatically as a function of being human. Since we can't turn off the meaning-making process, the key question becomes: how can we turn our disempowering stories into stories that increase our possibilities and enrich our lives? What we want to unleash is the power of a good story.

8

Creating Empowering Stories

If our suffering lies primarily in the meaning that we give to what happened, and if we have the power to assign meaning, then we are empowered to change the meaning that we create. We are the authors of the stories that we tell ourselves. We are the authors and therefore, if we so choose, we can create the world so that we experience the world differently.

Notice the subtle shift that I am pointing to here. I am not saying that we create a different world. Instead, I am saying that we are always interacting with the world that we experience rather than an absolute world. We experience the world through our perceptions which are assembled in our brain through selection, interpretation, and categorization. If we change the focus of our selection, interpretation, and categorization, we will change how we perceive the world.

I find it interesting that, at this point, some people will object by saying that creating an empowering story is just make-believe; it is not the truth. I understand how this step can feel uncomfortable because I went through this doubt myself. However, we can realize that we have been living inside of stories all along, but have just not been aware of it.

When our meaning-making machinery is hidden behind the veil of our unconscious mind, we easily make up stories and then believe

Creating Empowering Stories

that they are true. Now, when we attempt consciously to create an empowering story, we are all of a sudden aware of making up a story and it feels strange or artificial. The meaning-making machinery is exposed, like the Wizard of Oz, and appears to be a charlatan.

What we really need in order to take this step towards empowerment, is to get present to our meaning-making process behind our disempowering stories. These stories are not true either! In both cases the stories are made up. We are faced with a choice, but not between truth and falsehood since both kinds of stories are created in our minds. Rather, we can choose to stay with our disempowering stories that limit us and keep us victims or we can choose to live from our empowering stories that create unlimited possibility for our lives.

Opening up New Possibilities

Look back at the two stories that I related in Chapter One. Sara and Heather experienced two very different worlds: one was a sad and lonely world and the other was full of possibility. I told you that both of these stories are my stories. Now perhaps you can see that the "Sara" story is a disempowering way of framing my childhood, whereas the "Heather" story creates an empowering framework: "I can be anything I choose to be."

I didn't need to change any of the facts of my childhood to create an empowering story. All I did was to change which aspects of my childhood I chose to focus on, and the meaning that I created from these experiences. I had the power within me to make either one of these stories the truth for me by following through with one and dropping the language of the other.

A friend of mine told me about his experience of creating an empowering story. He was in a public library, and there was a young man sitting near him who was playing a computer game. My friend could hear the music from the game and also various noises that the young man made in his enthusiasm over the game.

My friend was starting to be annoyed by how inconsiderate this young man was of others around him. However, he realized that he was creating a story about this young man, and chose to create a different story rather than ruin his day being distracted by both the young man and by his own story of the young man. My friend created a story that the young man was so absorbed in enjoying his game that he was unaware of the noise he was making. My friend happily returned to his own work and was not disturbed any further.

Notice that neither the disempowered story nor the empowered story required knowing anything about the young man. My friend simply reframed how the young man occurred to him in his own mind; he changed how he experienced the young man. This is a good enough reframe in itself. The icing on the cake came a little while later when another person approached the young man and proceeded to have a conversation with him – in sign language! My friend realized that the young man was deaf and wasn't able to hear the sounds coming from his computer to realize the disturbance it was causing.

Using Stories to Create our Future

The stories we tell about our own lives are powerful frameworks for viewing the world. Our personal stories shape our lives. We actually live forward into the story of who we say we are. These stories will shape our sense of identity, how we interact with others, how we experience the world, and the possibilities we see for ourselves in our lives.

To regain our empowerment, we have an opportunity to create stories that open up new possibilities, "re-frame" a situation, or re-tell our story to our self from a different framework. We can even re-create our own past by the way we tell our history to our self and to others. For example, instead of casting our self in the victim role, we could choose to use a framework that casts our self in the hero role.

Rather than telling a "poor me" story, we can tell a "fortunate me" story.

An example of re-telling a story that creates a new possibility of what the world can look like can be found in this quote from the poem "Outwitted" by Edwin Markham: "He drew a circle that shut me out…. But Love and I… drew a circle that took him in."[1] A change in perception, changes the way that we experience the world.

At any time, we can create an empowering story that opens up new possibilities for our life. Possibilities define the framework of what we want to create. For example, Carol created the story of the possibility of Martin being the perfect partner for her. A friend of mine who retired recently created a story of the possibil-

---

[1] The Shoes of Happiness and Other Poems (1913) http://www.archive.org/stream/shoeshappines00markrich/shoeshappines00markrich_djvu.txt

ity of traveling around the country to meet inspiring people. He then lived into this story as the truth about his life. Another friend created the story of the possibility of ease at work and she lived into this story by taking charge of her calendar to create the spaciousness that she wanted.

You might say that this is just making a plan or setting an intention and acting on it; there is nothing new here. You are partially right. What I am pointing to here is listening to the internal story and addressing that. Very often people make plans and don't follow through or sabotage their own plans by telling themselves, "This is stupid; I can't really do this; I can't really afford to do this; great idea, but it will never work;" etc. These are the stories I am talking about that can to be brought into awareness and alignment with possibility, just like Carol had to change her inner story, "He is wrong for me" to create a possibility of a meaningful relationship.

When we create an empowering story based on possibility, the brain will set off to solve this problem and find an answer. It will look for evidence to support the possibility. It will line up the support and resources we need to make it work. If we tell the brain that what we want is <u>not</u> possible, it will comply and support THAT story in just the same way. Each of us can choose which story we want to tell our brain and our brain will comply by supporting that story.

Empowerment and Positive Thinking

I want to make a distinction between retelling our story to create empowerment and possibility versus what has been called "positive thinking." While these two strategies have some elements in common, they are not the same.

An example of positive thinking might be something like this: "Every day I feel better and better." There is nothing wrong with positive thinking and many people have been helped in their lives through using positive thinking. However, reframing or retelling our story goes a step or two beyond positive thinking by using what is now understood about the episodic aspect of the human brain.

Using our story-telling skills, we can go beyond and expand the above example of positive thinking by:

- looking into our past to see how this is true,

- finding all the examples in the past of how we actually have felt better each day,

- telling that story to ourselves, and

- noticing and telling ourselves and others how we are feeling better each day.

By creating a story around the positive thought, we will begin to use the power of story-telling to give the brain instructions to notice the evidence that supports this story of feeling better every day.

But the process must go deeper than this so that we do not ignore or deny messages that are counter to the positive story: messages that we also need to pay attention to for our well-being. The story-telling process I am describing in this book is not just an insistence that everything is better and better each day, especially when some aspects are clearly not better.

Creating Empowering Stories

How can we reconcile using a positive statement when our experience is not positive? If we stay with affirming the positive, then we risk living disconnected from our experience, which is not desirable. On the other hand, if we affirm the negative experience, we risk staying in our suffering, which is equally not desirable.

The answer to this dilemma lies in working with separating observation and interpretation thereby becoming aware of the meaning-making and stories that we create. When there is something related to our well-being that needs our attention, we can learn to focus on the observation without creating extra drama or added meaning around it. In other words, we can eliminate the suffering about the suffering and focus on what is actually happening instead of on our story about what is happening. When we focus on what is actually occurring, we can choose more easily which actions we can take to remedy the situation the best we can.

For example, if you break your arm, most likely you will need to get someone to drive you to an urgent care center. Chanting, "Every day I feel better and better," will not mend your broken arm. However, chanting "Woe is me" won't mend your broken arm either! If you reduce the drama around how you react to circumstances in your life, you will indeed feel better and better! Similarly, if you begin to notice that a relationship you are in leaves you feeling disconnected with yourself or unhappy, you have the power to take responsibility for your well-being and to choose what you want to do about it. Neither trying to convince yourself that it is getting better nor complaining to your friends about how awful it is will accomplish much of anything.

Reframing a Disempowering Story

How can we tell a positive story when seemingly negative things are occurring in our world? Remember that our brain selects, interprets and categorizes input and that situations are inherently neutral until we give them meaning.

I recently submitted an article for possible publication in a journal. I received back a letter saying, "We cannot accept this article in its current form without significant revision." The meaning I made up was, "My article was rejected."

When I talked to a colleague about this, she said that she had never had an article published that didn't first have to go through revisions. My friend helped me to reframe the "rejection" letter into, "We will accept your article after you make a few revisions." When I read my "rejection" letter again and the comments from the reviewers, I then saw that there were specific suggestions for revisions that were not all that difficult to do. I did make the revisions and the article was accepted for publication.

Here is an example that goes through the process of reframing a negative situation. Something negative happens: you are in a fender-bender accident on the way to work and you miss an important meeting because of it. Two "whammies" in one! How is it possible to create an empowering story out of this? First of all, it might be useful to notice the disempowering story that may already be running in your mind. This disempowering story would sound like:

- blaming the other driver,

Creating Empowering Stories

- worry over how much damage has been done to your car and how much that will cost and how short you are on money already this month and where is the money going to come from for the xyz that you were planning to buy,

- anger over having to spend time sorting all of this out rather than getting to the important meeting, and

- anxiety about what will occur in the meeting in your absence.

- Poor me!

Let's see how we can turn this all around by slowing down the process and first, clearly identifying the observations and second, choosing empowering interpretations.

Observation: My car hit the car in front of me at a stop light. What else do I remember about what happened? The car in front started to move forward and then quickly stopped. I also started to move forward but did not put on my brakes before I bumped into the car in front of me. Oh yes! I remember now that I saw a bicyclist crossing the road in front of the first car.

Interpretation: The driver in front of me must have seen the bicycle after he started moving forward and then stepped on the brake to avoid hitting the bicycle. Wow! I am glad he saw the bicycle in time to stop! This could have been much worse than a couple of bent fenders!

Observation: It is 10:15am and my meeting starts in 15 minutes.

Interpretation: It may take longer than 15 minutes to process this accident and I will probably be late to the meeting.

Observation: I am on the agenda for the meeting to lead a planning conversation about an event for tomorrow.

Interpretation: This event planning is important and needs to happen at this meeting. I am responsible for this going well. I had better let my assistant know I will not be there and ask him to lead the conversation in my place. Actually, this is perfect because I have been wanting to give him an opportunity to take the lead and be more visible for the contribution he makes.

Observation: The damage is all on my car and nothing on the other car. The other driver agrees that his car is fine. I have insurance with a $500 deductible. I am low on cash this month because I had planned to purchase the xyz.

Interpretation: The damage is probably less than $500 so it would have to be repaired out of my money. I really want the xyz but I could wait to buy it, or I could wait to repair the minor damage to my car for another month. Either way, I am okay and I can choose which expense I want to incur first.

Observation: The other driver apologized for slamming on his brakes and explained about the bicycle. He checked the damage on his car and said there was no damage. He asked if I was all right.

Interpretation: The other driver is really nice and considerate. This probably isn't going to take as long as I thought. I might even make it to the last part of the meeting. What a relief!

Creating Empowering Stories

What a different outcome from this set of interpretations than the previous "poor me" story!

I am not saying that you should expect to be able to turn around a disempowering story on the spot. It takes practice doing many post-game analyses to learn how to work with your story-making process before you will be able to do some of it in the moment. However, when you are able to slow down your mental process and separate out the observations and interpretations as illustrated in this example, I think that you will find it much easier to empower yourself with the way that you interpret the events you encounter in your life.

One powerful way to practice reframing is to take a situation that happened in the past and ask yourself how many different ways you could tell this story and still explain the same facts. For example, you could think of how you would tell the story to different audiences. It might even be helpful for you to write down or record the story again and again in the way that you would tell it to your mother; your best friend; your boss; your psychotherapist; your spiritual counselor; on your first date with someone; to a complete stranger on an airplane; and at a job interview.

My guess is that you will have many different versions of the same situation after you do this. All of the stories are true…and not the Truth. Once you see this for yourself in a situation from your own life you will then be able to question the stories that you are telling and ask if they are empowering or disempowering for you.

You can tell when you are entangled in a disempowering story whenever you feel a loss of energy, feel stuck, or feel like a victim. On the contrary, when you are in an empowering story, you will more likely experience some or all of the following: feel energized, see a clear path to action, feel at peace, have several good options to choose from, feel open to possibilities, and feel forgiving of yourself and others.

A teacher I know uses this technique to be open to an empowering outcome: he invites a solution by saying to himself, "There will be a way through this." Another practice you can use to build awareness and empowerment is to ask these questions whenever you become aware that you are stuck in a disempowering story.

- When you feel a loss of power or self-worth, what story are you telling yourself in that precise moment?

- In what aspect of the story you are telling do you feel a loss of power?

- Is there another way you could tell the story that would feel more empowering?

I have a friend who is famous for approaching difficult situations by asking the question: "How is this just perfect?" Asking this question will set the brain off searching for an appropriate answer, and it will likely find several credible responses. The human brain is designed to answer the questions we pose to it.

For example, Joe has just been fired from his job. How is this just perfect? Joe might realize any of the following possibilities is true for him:

- He wasn't happy on the job, and losing his job gives him the time to find something he would enjoy more.

- He had been thinking about going back to school, but felt like he owed it to his job to stick with it instead. Now he doesn't have to worry about that and can pursue his educational goal.

- He is confused about how this happened. He thought he had been doing a good job, but being fired might mean that he wasn't interpreting the signals correctly. This is a good opportunity to reflect on how he approached his job, his boss, and co-workers. Maybe there is something he can learn from this experience that will help him in his next job.

As with most transformative processes, it sometimes takes time to change our habitual patterns and to hold with compassion the parts of us that still believe and behave in the old ways. While we work on reframing our stories, we also may need to use other methods that help stuck places in us to develop. Meditation, Inner Relationship Focusing, Tonglen, Somatic Experiencing, and The Work are some examples of tools that can support the development of old, stuck patterns.

From Personal to Global

I have been speaking primarily about changing the story at a personal level. However, the same principles can be applied to changing a family, cultural, ethnic, organizational, national, or global story. We can begin to notice when disempowering stories are restricting the possibility for positive change.

One example of a collective disempowering story is the "against" movements; against war, against pollution, against crime. "Against" movements focus people's energy on what they don't want, which commonly only increases the instances of what they don't want. You have probably heard the saying, "what we resist, persists."

Once we notice that we ourselves and others around us are operating from a disempowered story, we can invite others to join us in reframing the story. Instead of focusing on what we don't want, it is immensely more powerful to ask these questions:

- What do we want more of?

- How are we when we are at our best?

- What are some specific examples of when things worked in the way we enjoyed?

- How do we want things to look five years from now?

Through jointly addressing these questions, we can collaboratively create a story that is empowering, opens up a new range of possibilities, and gives us a positive way to live into the future. We can find ways to inspire others to positive action through telling a new story.

Great leaders, like Martin Luther King Jr., have been able to inspire powerful movements through creating a story, or a "dream," full of possibility and hope. Telling a story about what we want more of in our life, and inviting people to put their energy towards creating THAT, will most likely increase the instances of exactly what we want. Many people will collectively live into this new story through their actions, thus creating a movement of positive change. This is the basis for wide-scale grassroots change.

Creating Empowering Stories

I recently discovered an example of storytelling to create a positive future in an article called "A National Strategic Narrative."[2]

This narrative (story) describes a new role in the world for the United States, a role that creates new possibilities for global relationships. I quote a small section here as an example of creating an empowering story that calls forth possibility on a global level. More than the content (which you may or may not agree with), notice the use of language in this quote to create a positive statement of what is desired. Notice how the authors paint a picture through narrative of a possibility for the future that can call people into creating this future.

---

[2] Mr. Y (2011),, Woodrow Wilson International Center for Scholars
http://www.wilsoncenter.org/sites/default/files/A%20National%20Strategic%20Narrative.pdf?inf_contact_key=346ecc0dfe52d43015055410a83b7ed071a0d1f80c5ccc5ece1e3cf256ccb47d

> This Narrative advocates for America to pursue her enduring interests of prosperity and security through a strategy of sustainability that is built upon the solid foundation of our national values. As Americans we needn't seek the world's friendship or to proselytize the virtues of our society. Neither do we seek to bully, intimidate, cajole, or persuade others to accept our unique values or to share our national objectives. Rather, we will let others draw their own conclusions based upon our actions. Our domestic and foreign policies will reflect unity of effort, coherency and constancy of purpose. We will pursue our national interests and allow others to pursue theirs, never betraying our values. We will seek converging interests and welcome interdependence. We will encourage fair competition and will not shy away from deterring bad behavior. We will accept our place in a complex and dynamic strategic ecosystem and use credible influence and strength to shape uncertainty into opportunities. We will be a pathway of promise and a beacon of hope, in an ever changing world.

This narrative was created by two individuals who empowered themselves to share their positive vision of global relationships. Likewise, we can empower ourselves to share our visions with our communities of influence. Articulating an empowering vision can have the effect of aligning others in a common direction.

Others may have similar values, hopes, and dreams that remain private or disempowered. When one person steps out to provide language around a positive story, others become empowered to live into that story. I can imagine that this is the meaning intended in the following quote, attributed to Margaret Mead, "Never doubt that a small group of thoughtful, committed citizens can change the world. Indeed it is the only thing that ever has."

9

Happiness is a Good Story

I am hoping that this title now means something new or more for you than it did at first. By "story," I am referring to the interpretation and meaning that we create about our life, our self, and other people that impacts the way that we experience the world. I am hoping that you can now see and understand the co-creative role that you play in your own story.

I define a "good" story as one that is empowering, that creates our self as an active agent, with freedom and choice to take ownership of our creative power, even when "bad" things happen. Now I want to connect a "good story" to achieving happiness.

We can sometimes receive messages from various sources, spiritual teachings, self-help books, friends and relatives, to "be happy." There may not be any tools that come with the message that give us access to happiness. Or worse, the message may come loaded with lots of judgment and unsolicited advice. The question often remains, though, how to access happiness when you are not happy. The key question is, what is it that gives us access to happiness?

Just as suffering comes from our thoughts and the meaning that we give to our circumstances, so is happiness the result of our meaning-making. When we interpret our experiences in ways that give them positive meaning and create possibility for ourselves

Happiness is a Good Story

and others, we create the basis for happiness in our lives. In order to do this, we need to be able to notice our perspective and shift from negative interpretations to positive interpretations. We need to develop the ability to see a range of possibilities rather than limit our focus to just one interpretation.

In order to develop the skill of generating happiness, it is important to learn to take charge of our thoughts and meaning-making process. We are used to our thought processes occurring in the background and at the edge of consciousness. We normally don't pay much attention to our thoughts as they occur and we usually aren't aware of the potential consequences of our thoughts.

Most of us were not taught the power of our thoughts to create the quality of our lives. When we begin to see the meaning-making process that occurs in our minds, we can begin to take responsibility for our thoughts and the consequences that they create in how we experience our world. The suggestions I have given in this book for creating an empowering story provide powerful tools for taking charge of the meaning-making process.

Happiness is a natural result of empowerment. Certainly we can agree that playing the victim role, feeling stuck, and having no choice in our lives generally are not the substance of happiness. We can also all point to examples of people who have endured tremendously difficult circumstances that they could not change, and yet they have still found access to happiness.

When we cannot change our circumstances, we still have power over our thoughts and the stories that we tell ourselves about our circumstances. I am reminded of Viktor Frankl's observation, in his book *Man's Search for Meaning*[3], that the people in a concentration camp who were able to survive their own despair were those who found a way to <u>make meaning</u> of their lives even in these dire circumstances.

When we are able to change from a disempowering story to an empowering story, it can be like a "mountain top" experience: our problems can simply disappear with the new view that we have of the world. We can think that everything has changed, but then the old story, the old thoughts may come back again.

There may be a period of time when we flip back and forth between the old story and the new story. When this happens, we may just

---

[3] Frankl, V. E. (2006). Man's search for meaning. Boston: Beacon Press.

need to hold the parts of us that still believe the old story with compassion, and without judgment or resistance. While we continue forward with our empowering stories, we can also gently listen to these stuck parts for a while, like we would a young child, until these stuck parts of us change in their own time.

A Hero's Story

One key to happiness is to create a story of yourself and your life which puts you in the hero role. The hero of the story is able to assess the circumstances and find a way through, despite all sorts of setbacks, villains, obstacles, and challenges. The hero is not swayed; the hero does not believe the naysayers who say the path is impossible or impassable. The hero does not accept or believe any story of himself or herself as too weak, too small, or too inexperienced to undertake the challenge, even though there may be moments of doubt or being overwhelmed. No wonder we tend to love epic stories of good overcoming evil!

As I write this, I am thinking of the Star Wars epic or the Hobbit trilogy which both tell a story about unlikely heroes. And yet even these heroes were able to fulfill their role and save the day. We, too, can create our own epic story of overcoming the odds and contributing in ways that we previously didn't imagine that we could. Happiness is within reach of our own story-making.

May the power of your imagination lead you to create stories that bring you joy and happiness. Or to paraphrase a saying from Star Wars: May the force of a good story be with you!

Harmony World Publishing

Harmony World Publishing is dedicated to facilitating the development of world peace and the advancement of human communication and relationships through publishing books, articles, blogs, and other written materials. The Japanese word for harmony, Aiki, is the ability to harmonize with an opponent's energy and is one of the essential qualities for a traditional Japanese warrior. This principle of Aiki is essential in political, business, and social leaders as well as in families, schools, and social activism. The promotion of world harmony requires strength, commitment, inner discipline, and courage. Harmony is the opposite of domination of one person, group, or idea over another. The ability to relate effectively with people of diverse cultures and perspectives is a hallmark of harmony as is the ability to find solutions through collaboration and dialogue that meet everyone's needs. There is a need in our world for increasing the skills of people at all levels to facilitate peace building activities and communication. To this end, Harmony World Publishing promotes materials that support the development of understanding and skillfulness in facilitating peace.

website: www.harmonyworld.net

Taking Charge of Your Spiritual Path. For both those who have found a spiritual home and for those who are still looking, there is a need for spiritual seekers to have a better understanding of the process and principles of spiritual development. If you want to do practices that have meaning for you and to be able to change your practice when something more or different is needed, this book will provide you with some basic principles to help you take charge of your own spiritual path. People are taking more responsibility for managing their own finances, their own psychological well-being, and their own education. Likewise, it is possible now to take charge of one's own spiritual path. In most spiritual paths, the outcomes are often not made clear and the focus is placed on the practice itself without making the objective of the practice clear. This is disempowering for you, the practitioner. But now, we no longer have to stay stuck in this model. The purpose of this book is to identify some common underlying objectives of true spiritual practices outside of the doctrine that surrounds them. This book discusses the specific outcomes that different practices are designed to accomplish. ISBN 978-0-9911-1171-8

...the Professional Series

Empathy in Conflict Intervention: The Key to Successful NVC Mediation. The focus of this book is on mediation, a third party intervention role that can be undertaken by supervisors, managers, human resource professionals, marriage and family therapists, teachers, mediators, peace keepers, and parents. The authors make a strong case for the central role of empathy in promoting a successful mediation, especially when ongoing relationships between the parties are at stake. This book provides a thoughtful study of the important role of empathy in mediation through the development of a theoretical model to explain the effectiveness of Nonviolent Communication™ (NVC) mediation. The theory building process used in this book, as well as the list of conditions for a successful mediation, can be broadly applied to other third party intervention methods. ISBN 978-1-4776-1460-0

Available now at www.harmonyworld.net.

About the Authors

Nelle Moffett and Rick Bowers are married to each other and have a consulting company, Speak Peace, through which they lead workshops, facilitate practice groups and coach individuals, parents, couples, and businesses in communication and conflict resolution using Marshall Rosenberg's Nonviolent Communication™.

Nelle Moffett, Ph.D., spent 25 years in higher education as a strategic planner, researcher, change agent, coach, and internal consultant. She received her doctoral degree in Educational Leadership and Policy Studies from Arizona State University. She has taught Psychology courses at California State University Channel Islands. Nelle is a certified Life Coach and certified teacher of Inner Relationship Focusing. Nelle received training in communication skills from Landmark Education and the Center for Nonviolent Communication. Nelle is a long-time student of life, spirituality, philosophy and psychology.

Email: moffett@speak-peace.com.

Rick Bowers, M.A., Rick spent twenty-six years with Hewlett-Packard Company, primarily in Research and Development. In 2007 he left Hewlett-Packard to obtain a Master's Degree in Conflict Analysis and Engagement at Antioch University Midwest. He has mediated in the courts in Ventura and LA counties in California. Rick received training in communication skills from Landmark Education and the Center for Nonviolent Communication.

Email: bowers@speak-peace.com.

www.ingramcontent.com/pod-product-compliance
Lightning Source LLC
Chambersburg PA
CBHW061444040426
42450CB00007B/1204